Follow Me Around™
Canada

By Wiley Blevins

SCHOLASTIC

Consultant: Munroe Eagles, PhD, Professor and Director of Canadian Studies, University at Buffalo, Buffalo, New York

Library of Congress Cataloging-in-Publication Data
Names: Blevins, Wiley, author.
Title: Canada / by Wiley Blevins.
Description: New York : Children's Press, An Imprint of Scholastic Inc., 2018. |
Series: Follow me around | Includes bibliographical references and index.
Identifiers: LCCN 2017000113 | ISBN 9780531237083 (library binding : alk. paper) | ISBN 9780531239742 (pbk. : alk. paper)
Subjects: LCSH: Canada—Juvenile literature.
Classification: LCC F1008.2 .B59 2018 | DDC 971—dc23
LC record available at https://lccn.loc.gov/2017000113

Design: Judith Christ Lafond & Anna Tunick Tabachnik
Text: Wiley Blevins
© 2018 Scholastic Inc.

1 2 3 4 5 6 7 8 9 10 R 27 26 25 24 23 22 21 20 19 18

Photographs ©: cover boy: Pauline St. Denis/Corbis/VCG/Getty Images; cover background: Orchidpoet/iStockphoto; back cover: Pauline St. Denis/Corbis/VCG/Getty Images; 1: Pauline St. Denis/Corbis/VCG/Getty Images; 3: JJS-Pepite/iStockphoto; 4: Pauline St. Denis/Corbis/VCG/Getty Images; 6 left: Felix Choo/Alamy Images; 6 top right: Radharc Images/Alamy Images; 6 bottom right: benedek/iStockphoto; 7 right: Miles Ertman/Media Bakery; 7 left: Wayne R Bilenduke/Getty Images; 8 left: Swissmargrit/Dreamstime; 8 center: Marilyn Angel Wynn/Getty Images; 8 background: Fudio/iStockphoto; 8 right: Martiapunts/Dreamstime; 9 top left: Stephen Mcsweeny/Shutterstock; 9 bottom left: CBW/Alamy Images; 9 right: KidStock/Media Bakery; 10 left: Marie-Reine Mattera/Getty Images; 10 right: Marie-Reine Mattera/Corbis/age fotostock; 11: AnatoliYakovenko/Thinkstock; 12 man: Svetlana Klimovich/Shutterstock; 12 frog: weervector/Shutterstock; 12-13 background: Vadim Yerofeyev/Dreamstime; 13 right: Renault Philippe/age fotostock; 13 left: Aji Pebriana/Shutterstock; 14 left: IMNATURE/iStockphoto; 14 right: Schoening/picture-alliance/dpa/AP Images; 15 left: Robert Chiasson/age fotostock; 15 right: Adwo/Shutterstock; 16 left: Michael Runkel/age fotostock; 16 top right: Renault Philippe/age fotostock; 16 bottom right: Bruce Corbett/Alamy Images; 17 top left: David Nunuk/Getty Images; 17 top right: Grant Faint/Getty Images; 17 bottom: JJS-Pepite/iStockphoto; 18 left: North Wind Picture Archives/Alamy Images; 18 center: North Wind Picture Archives/Alamy Images; 18 right: Universal History Archive/Getty Images; 19 left: REUTERS/Alamy Images; 19 right flag: Brothers Good/Shutterstock; 19 right sky: sumroeng chinnapan/Shutterstock; 20 top: Joe_Potato/iStockphoto; 20 bottom: Dave Fleetham/age fotostock; 21 top left: age fotostock/Alamy Images; 21 right: Michael Wheatley/Getty Images; 21 bottom left: mark peterson/Getty Images; 22 right: altrendo travel/Getty Images; 22 left: Photawa/iStockphoto; 23 center left: Richard Nowitz/Getty Images; 23 top left: Marc Dufresne/iStockphoto; 23 bottom left: Carlos Osorio/Getty Images; 23 top right: Jim Wilson/The New York Times/Redux; 23 center right: Wolfgang Kaehler/Getty Images; 23 bottom right: NurPhoto/Getty Images; 24: Trevor Lush/Media Bakery; 25 left: Avstraliavasin/Dreamstime; 25 right: Bettmann/Getty Images; 26 top: NASA images/Shutterstock; 26 bottom left: UpdogDesigns/iStockphoto; 26 bottom right: Ron Garnett/age fotostock; 27 bottom left: Vadim.Petrov/Shutterstock; 27 bottom right: Miles Ertman/Getty Images; 27 top: Wayne Lynch/Getty Images; 28 A: Gunter Marx Photography/Getty Images; 28 B: Design Pics Inc/Alamy Images; 28 C: Robert McGouey/Alamy Images; 28 D: Randy Lincks/Getty Images; 28 E: Joel W. Rogers/Getty Images; 28 F: José Fuste Raga/age fotostock; 28 G: Pete Ryan/Media Bakery; 30 top left: Lukasz Stefanski/Shutterstock; 30 top right: MargaretClavell/iStockphoto; 30 bottom: Pauline St. Denis/Corbis/VCG/Getty Images.

Maps by Jim McMahon.

Table of Contents

Where in the World Is Canada?

Hello, or *bonjour*, from Canada! Those are the two ways we welcome people where I live. I'm Jackson, your tour guide. You're about to visit the second-largest country in the world.

Canada is located north of the United States. My country's name comes from *kanata*, a **Native** American word for "village." Many **First Nations** people already lived in Canada when explorers, hunters, and settlers came here from France, England, and other places. Today, my country is a fascinating mix of these many peoples and **cultures**.

Fast Facts:

- Canada is made up of 10 **provinces** (Alberta, British Columbia, Manitoba, New Brunswick, Newfoundland and Labrador, Nova Scotia, Ontario, Prince Edward Island, Quebec, and Saskatchewan) and three **territories** (Northwest Territories, Nunavut, and Yukon Territory).

- The Nunavut territory is the homeland of the Inuit people, a native group.

- Approximately 80 percent of Canadians live in a 100-mile (161-kilometer) ribbon along the southern border with the United States.

- Canada contains 50 percent of the world's freshwater lakes and 10 percent of the world's forests.

Newfoundland fishing village

Home in the Saskatchewan province

City of Toronto

Home Sweet Home

I am from Toronto, Canada. I live with my parents and little sister. Homes in Canada are very similar to those in the United States. Why is this? Many of the same groups of people settled in both Canada and the United States. They brought with them their unique styles of homes.

Our **motto** in Canada is "*A mari usque ad mare,*" which means "from sea to sea" in Latin. As you travel from coast to coast, you will see some differences in each city based on the groups of people who settled there. Some of our cities look like those in Europe, with giant stone churches and buildings. Others have modern-looking steel-and-glass structures.

Even though ice is cold, in an igloo, it actually works to trap heat. This makes the inside of the house warmer than the outside.

Igloo

Inside an igloo

You have to travel to some of our more remote areas to find homes that are truly different. For example, in the far north, you might see igloos, or snow houses. Ice block by ice block, these frozen homes with domed roofs were built to keep people warm during the brutal winters. These traditional homes were first built by the Inuits, who live in areas where no trees grow. They created igloos because there was no wood to build with. Today, it's easier to get wood and other supplies from other parts of the country. So most Inuits live in more modern homes. Some build wooden homes shaped like igloos. Others live in box-shaped homes painted in bright colors such as yellow, green, purple, or turquoise.

Poutine

Maple candy

Pemmican

Tourtiere

Let's Eat

You won't go hungry in Canada! Here we take french fries to the next level. Our version of this yummy food is called *poutine*. Imagine a plate of fries with cheese curds mixed in and brown gravy drizzled on top. This is one of our tastiest treats, and you're sure to love it!

Look at our country's flag and you'll see the maple leaf. This is a hint to another of our special foods. We like everything maple in Canada. What could be better than maple syrup over a steaming stack of pancakes? How about maple-flavored candy shaped like maple leaves? You can't eat just one!

We hunt a lot in Canada, so wild meat is very popular. People enjoy reindeer, bison, venison (from deer), boar, caribou, moose, goose, and rabbit. *Pemmican* is made from dried bison or moose meat mixed with melted fat and berries. It is a favorite food. So is *tourtiere*, a pie filled with meat, vegetables, and spices.

Seafood

Milk in a bag

Mac and cheese

Eating Like an Explorer

European **pioneers** in Canada had some eating habits that most people today would probably find strange. Many of these explorers dined on beaver tails and moose noses. Yuck! Their diets were so bad that some got **scurvy**, a disease that caused their teeth to fall out.

Canada has lots of water—we have oceans on three of our borders and numerous rivers and lakes. So we eat a lot of seafood, too. In Canada, you can enjoy oysters, clams, salmon, crabs, lobsters, sardines, and other sea creatures.

One thing that might surprise you in Canada is that our milk comes in bags, not cartons or jugs like in the United States. Another surprise is our potato chips. We love ketchup-flavored chips.

Never fear if you're not an adventurous eater. Macaroni and cheese is a favorite of most of my friends, and Canadians eat more of it than any other country in the world. You'll have no problem finding a gooey plate of cheesy pasta!

We study both French and English in our classes at school.

Off to School

In Canada, we start school in kindergarten and go to grade 12, just like in the United States. Our typical school year runs from August through June. One of the first things we learn in school is how to read and write. Since much of Canada is **bilingual**, many of us learn to read and write in both English and French. Or, as we say in school, "*anglais et français.*" This is useful because in some of our cities, including Montreal and Quebec, people mainly speak French.

My best *ami*, Pierre, is from a French-speaking family so I get to practice my French a lot when I'm at his house. I know all the food words!

ami

friend

One thing you might notice in Canada is that we spell some of our words in English differently from the way you do in the United States. For example, words like *colour* and *honour* have the letter *u*. We spell these words like they do in England. That makes sense because England ruled over Canada for a long time. We also call the last letter of the alphabet *zed* instead of *zee*.

Canadian English	American English
colour	*color*
honour	*honor*
flavour	*flavor*
neighbour	*neighbor*
centre	*center*
theatre	*theater*

English
in use

Counting to 10

Counting to 10 is important to know when you visit one of our French-speaking cities.

1	**un** *(un)*
2	**deux** *(duh)*
3	**trois** *(twah)*
4	**quatre** *(kat-ruh)*
5	**cinq** *(sank)*
6	**six** *(sees)*
7	**sept** *(set)*
8	**huit** *(weet)*
9	**neuf** *(nuhf)*
10	**dix** *(dees)*

TALL TALE FROM CANADA

In school, we love to read tall tales about settlers and explorers from long ago. My favorite is the tale of Mufferaw Joe.

The Tale of Mufferaw Joe

I tell ya, if ever a tale was true this one certainly is. Why I'd stake my name and reputation on it. You see, over in Ottawa there lived the biggest and strongest man I ever did see. Heave-hi, heave-ho, that man's name was Mufferaw Joe. And what this man did I ain't never seen before.

For starters, Big Joe needed to get from Ottawa to Mattawa. I tell ya what, that trip takes days. But not for Big Joe. He hopped in a boat and used his arms to paddle up that river in just one day. Oh, yes he surely did.

People around here were always talkin' about Big Joe's really big pet. A frog! That frog was bigger than a horse and barked like an angry dog. Oh, I tell ya I ain't never seen a frog like that. Big Joe would hop on that frog's back and ride it from town to town. There was no train on any track in all of Canada that could get there faster. Oh, you should have seen it. Heave-hi, heave-ho, the best man in Ottawa was Mufferaw Joe.

Big Joe was quite the worker, too. He would get so busy cuttin' down timber he'd work up a mighty sweat. That sweat would drip off him like a rainstorm. Yes, it did. One day Big Joe was workin' up around Carleton Place. He worked up such a sweat that water poured out of him and formed the rushin' Mississippi River.

Soon after, Big Joe was fishin' in Calabogie Lake. He jumped in and swam back and forth to catch the biggest bass you ever did see. One problem though, that bass was as cross-eyed as I am. When Big Joe took one look at that fish, he shouted, "I can't eat this!" He covered up the fish so high we now call that pile of dirt Mount Saint Pat. And that's the truth, if ever there was truth! Heave-hi, heave-ho, the best man in Ottawa was Mufferaw Joe.

Mufferaw Joe

CN Tower

Queen Street

Touring Canada

Toronto

Welcome to my city, Toronto. The largest city in Canada, it is located on the northern shore of Lake Ontario, one of the five Great Lakes. The city's name comes from a native word meaning "place of meeting." More than 2.6 million people live in Toronto. When you come here, you'll want to go first to the CN (Canadian National) Tower. Hop on the elevator and zip up to the Sky Pod for a 360-degree view of the city. If you're afraid of heights, avoid the glass floor that towers 112 stories in the air.

Next, stroll the streets of beautiful Toronto. But be sure to look up as you walk around. Why? You might spot a giant car with spinning wheels bursting out of a building on Queen Street. Or you might see half a cow sticking out of a building on King Street. Grab your camera and snap some photos!

Parliament buildings

A statue of Terry Fox

Ottawa: Capital City

In the eastern province of Ontario, on the beautiful Ontario River, is Canada's capital city, Ottawa. Its name comes from the native Algonquian word *adawe*, which means "to trade." Long ago, Ottawa was a huge fur-trading post. Now it's the site of our country's government. Make sure to stop and take a picture of the majestic Parliament buildings, where our laws are made.

Running Across the Country

Across from Parliament Hill in Ottawa, you can find a statue dedicated to Terry Fox, who lost a leg to cancer in 1977. To raise money for cancer research, Terry decided to run across Canada in 1980. He ran 3,339 miles (5,374 km). When Terry reached the city of Thunder Bay, Ontario, he got sick again and had to give up. He died just a few months later. Each year, people do the Terry Fox Run to raise money in his honor. I ran it last year with my mom and dad.

Old Montreal

Biodome

A monkey inside the Biodome

Other Fun Places

In such a big country, many great places are waiting for you to visit. One of my favorites is Montreal, the second-largest city in the country. It's a mostly French-speaking city. Tourists flock there because of the blend of cultures it offers. Canada was ruled by both France and England at different times in our history, so the mix of French and English cultures and languages is common.

After you receive a proper *bienvenue*, or welcome, go to Mont Royal. This park has an amazing view of the St. Lawrence River and surrounding area. Enjoy a walk on the cobblestone streets of Old Montreal to feel like you're stepping back in time. Also make sure you visit the Biodome. There you can experience a tropical rain forest under the partially transparent roof of this building. Inside, you'll see monkeys, capybaras, poison arrow frogs, and more.

Vancouver

Vancouver Aquarium

Travel to the west coast to see the sights of Vancouver, British Columbia, the country's third-largest city. Vancouver has one of the country's busiest **harbors**. It's a perfect place for a boat ride. Make sure you visit the giant totem poles that were made by the Squamish, a First Nations people. Then head over to Chinatown, where you'll spot golden dragons on the streetlights and lots of yummy food. If you have time, pay a visit to the aquarium. When it opened in 1956, it was Canada's first public aquarium.

While you're on the west coast, spend time in nature at the Pacific Rim National Park Reserve. There, you'll find plenty of trails and trees that are more than 1,000 years old.

Totem pole

Our Fascinating History

Thousands of years ago, First Nations people lived across what is now Canada. Many of these groups still live in Canada today. They continue to add to our rich history.

When Europeans began arriving in North America as early as 986 CE, the First Nations people taught them how to survive. In the 1500s, the French explored the St. Lawrence River and started settlements in the area. Around the same time, British explorers came to the area near the Hudson Bay. They also started

Timeline: Canada's History

12,000 years ago until present day

First Nations
The first settlers came to Canada, forming various nations across the continent.

1534-1700s

French Explorers and Settlers
French explorers, such as Samuel de Champlain in 1608, come to Canada and build settlements.

1610-1900s

British Settlement and Rule
Great Britain defeats France in a war in 1713, taking over most of eastern Canada.

1812

The War of 1812
The U.S. declares war on the Canadian British colonies. After the war, Canadians begin demanding more say in how the colonies are ruled.

settlements. The two countries began to fight over control of the land and its resources. The First Nations people were caught in the middle of these terrible conflicts. Eventually, Great Britain took over much of what is now Canada. On July 1, 1867, our country was born.

But after 1867 Canada was still tied to Great Britain. All of our laws had to be approved by the British Parliament. That ended in 1982 when Canada gained the right to make its own laws.

1867

Canada Is Born

The various parts of Canada (Canada East, Canada West, Nova Scotia, New Brunswick) join together to form one country.

1982

Canada Can Rule Itself

The Canadian Parliament no longer has to get approval from Great Britain for its laws.

1999

More Territories Added

Nunavut becomes the third territory in Canada.

Today

Modern Era

Canada continues to be a peaceful and productive country.

It Came From Canada

In addition to maple syrup, here are some other special things you'll find in Canada:

Did you know the jolly man from the North Pole is Canadian? That's right: Santa Claus is from my country! Every Christmas, one million letters are addressed to Santa Claus at his own Canadian postal code: H0H 0H0, North Pole, Canada.

The narwhal is a type of whale that lives in the Arctic Ocean. A unique thing about this Canadian creature is its large horn, which can be more than 10 feet (3 meters) long. This makes it look like a sea unicorn.

Inuits have a unique way of making music called throat singing. It's a combination of humming, buzzing, twanging, and other sounds. Usually, two singers face each other while performing. You can watch and enjoy this unique art form if you visit Nunavut, the traditional Inuit territory.

Rumor has it that a monster called Ogopogo lurks in the waters of Okanagan Lake in the province of British Columbia. (I still haven't seen it, though!) What's so special about this monster? Its name is pronounced the same way forward and backward!

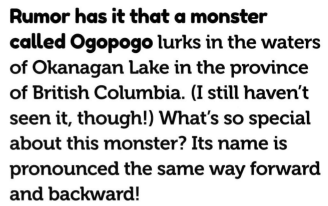

EXPLORE CANADA'S ARCTIC
12070N
NUNAVUT

The license plates in the Canadian territory of Nunavut are shaped like polar bears. Why? About half of the world's polar bears live there. People who live in Churchill leave their cars unlocked so that if anyone walking along the streets encounters a polar bear they will have a quick place to escape.

It's a Celebration!

Everyone loves a holiday, and we have some fun ones in Canada. The best, of course, is Canada Day. It began in 1867 when several provinces joined together to form the Dominion of Canada. That's what our country was first called. In fact, this holiday used to be called Dominion Day. We celebrate it on July 1 with parades, fireworks, fairs, and plenty of cookouts and barbecues.

Make a Canadian Wind Sock

You will need:

- Red and white acrylic paint
- Paintbrushes
- 1 empty soup can
- Red glitter
- Red and white ribbons
- Glue
- Hammer and nail
- String

Directions:

1. **Paint** the can white and wait for it to dry.

2. **Make** a red handprint on the can. **Sprinkle** glitter on the handprint.

3. **Paint** red rectangles on either side of the handprint to make it look like the Canadian flag.

4. **Cut** red and white ribbons and **glue** them to the bottom of the can. (Note: If you can get an adult to use a hot glue gun, the ribbons will stick better.)

5. **Punch** two holes in the top of the can using the hammer and nail. Then **thread** the string through and tie it in a knot. Use the string to hang the wind sock.

Winter Carnival
Held in Quebec, this celebration includes a famous canoe race across the St. Lawrence River.

St. Pierre Frog Follies
This celebration features a National Frog Jumping Championship. It's a hopping good time!

Winterlude
This popular outdoor festival is held in Ottawa. You'll see huge ice sculptures and people skating on the Rideau Canal.

Toonik Tyme
Held in April in Iqaluit, the capital of the Nunavut territory, this festival includes igloo building, traditional Inuit games, and big feasts.

Victoria Day
Held on the Monday before May 25, this holiday honors Queen Victoria, who once ruled Canada.

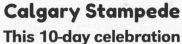

Calgary Stampede
This 10-day celebration will introduce you to everything western. Giddyap and yee-haw!

My friends and I play hockey every chance we get!

Time to Play

Sports are a popular pastime in Canada. It's cold much of the year here, so we especially love our winter sports—figure skating, skiing, snowshoeing, snowboarding (my favorite!), **curling**, and others. But nothing is loved as much as hockey. It's our national sport, along with lacrosse.

Lacrosse was invented by the Iroquois, a First Nations people. It involves using a small rubber ball and a long-handled stick. Teams run down the field and try to get the ball into a goal. If you play, be careful—a lot of body contact often happens in this rough sport. I've gotten a lot of bruises playing it!

Curling

One thing that might surprise you is that basketball was invented by a Canadian. We play this game a lot at school. Dr. James Naismith, who was from Ontario, created it when he wanted to make an indoor game for kids to play in the winter. He specifically wanted a game that required skill, not strength. The first basketball game was played with a soccer ball and peach baskets on each end of the court.

When the weather warms, we like to fish in our many lakes and hike along the scenic trails in our mountains and parks.

Dr. James Naismith

You Won't Believe This!

On February 3, 1947, in Snag, Yukon, in our northwestern territory, the temperature dipped to –81.4 degrees Fahrenheit (–63 degrees Celsius). That's about the same temperature as on Mars!

Off the coast of Newfoundland, you can spot icebergs. These large chunks of ice are broken pieces of Arctic **glaciers**. Some of the ice is 10,000 years old. Some of the icebergs can be as tall as skyscrapers—even though seven-eighths of the iceberg is usually under the water.

The Confederation Bridge reaches from New Brunswick to Prince Edward Island. It is 8 miles (13 km) long and one of the longest bridges in the world. It is so long and boring to drive across that a curve was built in to keep drivers awake.

The sand on the beaches of Prince Edward Island is not tan or white like on most beaches. Instead, it is red. Why? The sand is full of iron, which gets rusty and turns an orange-red shade when wet.

The northern lights, or aurora borealis, are a special treat in upper Canada from August through October. Here, winds collide with gases in the air. This releases energy that can be seen as dancing streams of color in the night sky. If you get a chance to see it, don't miss out. It's spectacular!

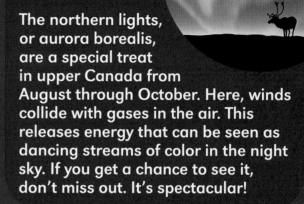

If you're in the Yukon Territory, go see Dawson City. This historic place looks just like it did during the gold rush of the late 1800s. Step back in time, grab a pan, and maybe you too will strike it rich!

Guessing Game!

Here are some other great sites around Canada. Can you guess which is which?

This museum has the largest collection of dinosaur skeletons in North America. **A**

1. Niagara Falls
2. Writing-on-Stone Provincial Park
3. Royal Tyrell Museum in Alberta
4. Albertosaurus in Drumheller
5. Capilano Suspension Bridge
6. Whistler Mountain
7. Big Muddy Badlands Hoodoos

B

These oddly shaped rocks, called hoodoos, are found in the province of Saskatchewan.

C

If you're looking for some more dinosaur fun, go here. You can even dig for fossils in the Fossil Discovery Center.

D

If your family loves to ski, this is the place! If it gets too cold, head indoors for even more fun things to do.

E

If you're feeling brave and want a spectacular view, visit this suspension bridge and enjoy the sights.

This is perhaps the most famous waterfall in North America (it borders the United States). But come to the Canadian side for the best view!

F

This park in Calgary has some of the earliest writing and drawing by Canada's First Nations people.

G

1F, 2G, 3A, 4C, 5E, 6D, 7B

Answer Key

28

How to Prepare for Your Visit

By now, you should be ready to hop on a plane (or get in a car) to Canada. Here are some tips to prepare for your trip.

1 Our money is called Canadian dollars. You'll need it to buy fun souvenirs. Our paper money is special: it has Braille-like markings for the blind. But don't look for pennies. We stopped making them several years ago. If you find a one-dollar coin, it's called a loonie. Now that's fun to say!

2 Bring a pair of binoculars. Canada has a diverse landscape—ice and snow, evergreen forests, rock-covered mountains, islands with sandy shores and green meadows, and plains filled with farmland. You're bound to see something you'll want to look at more closely. If you're on the coasts, be on the lookout for birds such as puffins and guillemots, which have distinctive red feet.

3 If you're looking for a bathroom in the French cities in Canada, remember this: *dames* are for girls and *hommes* are for boys. It's best to write this one down.

4 Canada is a great place for hiking. We have many forest and mountain trails through our 47 national parks. Some of these parks are larger than countries such as Denmark and Israel! Make sure you bring good walking boots, rain gear, bug repellant, a first-aid kit, snacks, and a change of clothing in case you get muddy or wet.

The United States Compared to Canada

	United States of America (USA)	Canada
Official Name	United States of America (USA)	Canada
Official Languages	No official language, though English is most commonly used	English and French
Population	325 million	35 million
Common Words	yes, no, excuse me, thank you	oui (we), non (non), excusez-moi (es-koo-zay mwah), merci (mare-see)
Flag		
Money	Dollar	Canadian dollar
Location	North America	North America
Highest Point	Denali (Mount McKinley)	Mount Logan
Lowest Point	Death Valley	Atlantic Ocean
National Anthem	"The Star-Spangled Banner"	"O, Canada"

So now you know some important and fascinating things about my country, Canada. I hope to see you someday playing hockey on one of our ice rinks, fishing in one of our lakes, or visiting one of our historic cities. Until then, as my friend from Montreal would say, *au revoir*! Good-bye!

Glossary

bilingual *(bye-LING-gwuhl)*
able to speak two languages well

cultures *(KUHL-churz)*
the customs and traditions of a group of people

curling *(KUR-ling)*
a sport where teams slide stones along ice to try and land them in a target

First Nations *(FURST NAY-shuhnz)*
native peoples that have lived in Canada since before the arrival of European settlers

glaciers *(GLAY-shurz)*
slow-moving masses of ice

harbors *(HAHR-burz)*
areas of calm water where ships can dock

motto *(MAH-toh)*
a short sentence that states someone's beliefs or is a rule for behavior

native *(NAY-tiv)*
relating to the people who were originally in a place

pioneers *(pye-uh-NEERZ)*
people who explore unknown territory and settle there

provinces *(PRAH-vin-sinz)*
regions of a country; Canada is divided into provinces like the United States is divided into states

scurvy *(SKUR-vee)*
a disease caused by a lack of vitamin C

territories *(TER-uh-tor-eez)*
areas connected with or owned by a country that are outside the country's main borders

Index

Facts for Now

Visit this Scholastic website for more information on Canada and to download the Teaching Guide for this series:

www.factsfornow.scholastic.com   Enter the keyword **Canada**

About the Author

Wiley Blevins lives and works in New York City. His greatest love is traveling, and he has been to Canada many times. He prefers visiting in the warmer summer months. Wiley has written numerous books for kids, including *Cinderella and the Vampire Prince, Ick and Crud: Mystery in the Barn*, and *Ninja Plants*.